Ukulele Music ◆ Perduta Gente

PETER READING

Ukulele Music

Perduta Gente

TRIQUARTERLY BOOKS
NORTHWESTERN UNIVERSITY PRESS

Evanston, Illinois

TriQuarterly Books
Northwestern University Press
Evanston, Illinois 60208-4210

Ukulele Music first published in Great Britain in 1985 by Martin Secker &
Warburg Limited. Copyright © 1985 by Peter Reading.

Perduta Gente first published in Great Britain in 1989 by Martin Secker &
Warburg Limited. Copyright © 1989 by Peter Reading.

Northwestern University Press/TriQuarterly Books edition published 1994
by arrangement with Reed International Books Ltd. All rights reserved.

Printed in the United States of America

ISBN 0-8101-5030-1 cloth
ISBN 0-8101-5005-0 paper

Library of Congress Cataloging-in-Publication Data

Reading, Peter.
    [Ukulele music - Perduta gente]
    Ukulele Music: Perduta gente / Peter Reading
      p. cm.
    "TriQuarterly books."
    ISBN 0-8101-5030-1 (cloth). — ISBN 0-8101-5005-0 (paper)
    1. City and town life—Poetry. 2. Violence—Poetry. I. Reading,
Peter. Perduta gente.
PR6068.E27U34 1994   94-11760
821'.914—dc20   CIP

The paper used in this publication meets the minimum requirements of the
American National Standard for Information Sciences—Permanence of Paper
for Printed Library Materials, ANSI Z39.48-1984.

Contents

Ukulele Music

Dear sir,

I come in this morning instead of tomorrow as I have to take ~~Budige budgie~~
Bird to the Vets, as he got out of cage door for the first time, By <u>accident</u>. As
I was putting seed in. & taking out sand sheet. He went mad. & banged
himself against THE wall. & fell down on to the Magic coal fire. got
jammed in the back of coal effect. Broken leg and side of his body awfull
state. he is in. good job fire was not on.

faithly Viv

p.S. could you oblige the next weeks money this wk. be in tomorrow
Morning, Only the Capting which I chars for tuesdays has let me off this
Tues but has PAID yrs Viv

'They must have been about 17/18, possibly 19:
one, tattooed on his hand MAM; one, tattooed on his arm LOVE.

One of them grabbed at my handbag but I just belted him with it,
caught him one under the ear, then I yelled "Somebody, help!"

Even although it was lunchtime and several people were
watching
nobody wanted to know. Two women just walked right past.'

She had been pushing her 8-month-old, Sharen-Jayne, in the
buggy.
Now the kid started to scrawk; one of our heroes smirked, spat,

fondled the empty pint bottle he had in his hand and then
smashed it
on an adjacent brick wall, held the bits to the child's throat.

'I said "Hurt me if you like but don't injure the innocent baby –
it can't defend itself, see? Don't do it don't do it *please*!"

He said "If I do the baby I'll get what I want, so I'll cut it."
He shoved the glass in her cheek; twisted the jagged edge in.

He told me "This is how we earn our living, this and the dole
like."
Then he just wiggled the sharp, smashed slivers into her eye.'

Promptly the mother gave over her golden wedding-ring, also
three pounds in cash and a watch (silver, engraved 'My True
Love'),

but the attackers slashed Sharen twice more – in the mouth, and a
deep cut
neatly round one chubby knee. Then they strolled leisurely off.

'Sharon was screaming and bleeding a lot and I thought they had
killed her.'

C.I.D. officers say 'This is a callous assault . . .'

Dear Sir,

will finish of your hoovering and such tomorrow as my hand is still bad, my right one. As last wk. there is a lady two doors off me has a bitch and a little boy over the road had been playing with it. and since then where all the dogs came from I do not know. But one of them had pinned the boy against the wall. I ran out with a hand full of pepper to throw at the dogs face. I throw it. but it had bit me in the hand. just above my right thumb where the bone is. I ran after the dog. with a whitening brush also and I fell also over the fence. bruised my knee's. But my knee is alright. My hand I have sufferd. The dog got put down to sleep. I have been to Hospitle But I heard later. that another dog had pinned the same boy he is only four yrs old. and MARLD him in the face and eyes he has had 5 stitches across his left eye. The other dog also had to be put down to sleep I tell you it has been awfull over there with the dogs. The woman who the bitch belongs to, had forgotten she had left her kitchen window open One of the dogs had jump in through the window. her Husband had delt with the dog. But slammed the kitchen window and all of the glass had fallen out in pieces. (It is awfull. when the little girls are about.) There mothers have to keep them in. or take them with them. the pain is going all the way up my arm. I have had a TECNAS. you know, a little RED CARD.

YRS Viv.

Someone has left a whole crateful of empty lemonade bottles
on the pedestrian bridge. Here come three ten-year-old boys.

Queuing for buses, the off-peak shoppers are gathered together
under the cast concrete span (aerosolled WANKERS and TREV).

Each of the children has picked up an empty and, quite
                                                nonchalantly,
hurls it down onto the grans, young mums and spinsters and
                                                        babes.

No one evinces surprise or alarm or even vexation,
fox-trotting through the smashed bits, Terpsichorean and deft.

Each boy throws four bottles, spits from the parapet into our
                                                     faces,
shouts 'Fucking bastards' and yelps. Glass crunches under a bus.

Blood smears the calf of an elderly lady silently weeping.
'Kids' our conductor observes 'should be done something about.'

Grans are bewildered by post-Coronation disintegration;
offspring of offspring of *their* offspring infest and despoil.

('You think you're doing a fine job of work don't you, oh yes, but
you're not. Stop it stop it, it's dirty dirty dirty in the streets like
that' an old woman shopper informs two boys of ten or eleven
who slouch against a butcher's window in busy Northcote Rd.,
SW11. Moist beige tripes gleam. Around the Chopper bikes blobs
of bubbly saliva streaked green and yellow describe a semi-circle
on the greasy pavement. The boys giggle and one of them remarks
sotto voce 'Fuck off old cow'. 'What did you say?' They giggle
and do not answer. One boy spits afresh at his colleague's cycle.
A glycerite sac depends from the canary-coloured spokes, elon-
gates gradually. 'Dirty little devils. Look at them look at them!'
she appeals to those of us nearby. We evince neither surprise nor
concern. She turns begrudgingly. Silver streaks jet concurrently
from gaps between the front teeth of each boy. She continues
upon her way unaware that her pink leatherette mac is sullied by
twin viscid drools.)

Stubbornly, Taffs, at their damn-fool anachronistic eisteddfods,
still, with this breach in the hull, twang (ineffectual lyres).

Mercury falls, it's no go, and the pink geraniums shrivel:
ceilidh and Old Viennese drone as the packet goes down.

When all the cities were felled by the pongoid subspecies in them
(Belfast, Jerusalem, Brum., Liverpool, Beirut) and when

blood-swilling (Allah is wonderful) Middle-East Yahoos had
                                                    purchased
nuclear hardware, he found distich the only form apt.

Too Many Of Us and Dwindled Resources and War had undone
                                                         us.
Matter impartially throve (quark, strangeness, charm) not as *us*.

Sing in Your Bath if You Want to Seem Sexy and **Blood-Bath
                                               in Jordan**
vie for front page in the tabs. Doh ray me fah soh lah te

well, Sir

Only, the Capting has said I was not really wanted so I have gone to you instead. only. You are not here as you know. So have let myself in with spare key but he has PAY me just the same as he is kind old man with heart of gold etc. and has told me how underneath. and he has seen it with OWN eyes so knows it is true. where I thought it was just Underground Car Park ect. under ~~Civic~~ Civet Centre is not just Car Park but bunk for FALL if there is trouble, that sometimes seems likely with uSA and russiens with there bomb warfair. but what can you do? nothing and he say there are SARDINES stored in there for after siren. with DRINK. so we are all prepared thank God. But what I want to know is when you vote the different Goverments do NOT do what you ask do they? Because I want NO TROUBLE but it seems no difference what you want the Rulers just do a DIFFERENT THING. So you can only keep CHEERFUL and keep trying your best. sir. for Exsample I have done the floors but their is one of Yr writings there that ALAS is swept in the Hoover bag, and I got it out all right but is VERY twisted with the thing that BEATS as SWEEPS as CLEANS the one about a Piano and Man AND woman that I think is DIRTY but it takes all sorts and did you REALLY work at such a club in uSA? I never knew you had been there but I would not want sardines ALL THE TIME who would? noone. but it would be emergency like in the last one where it was tin sheeting. But now they are on the streets the ARMY against thugs and Mugers as that is where the REAL war is on NOW, cities in 2 halfs with police and army and nice folks against dirty animals, so may HAVE to go DOWN soon for THAT war. But I have throw it away, the poetry writing on the Piano at top of kitchin bin VERY TOP if you want it back.

and Oblige Viv.

Beetrooty colonels explain to the Lounge Bar how, in the 'Last
                                                          Show',
they had a marvellous time, and how we need a new war

if we are going to get this Great Country back on its feet, sir
(also all beards should be shaved: also the Dole should be
                                                          stopped).

Life still goes on and *It isn't the end of the world* (the child-soothing
platitudes weaken now Cruise proves them potentially false).

Lieder's no art against these sorry times (anguished Paramour
                                                          likens
mountainy crags and a crow to the flint heart of his Frau).

Dear sir,

have done some hoover of the front room. but am going now be back tomorrow morning if you can oblige with next week money same as last time. Only my sister. not the one in Australia the other one here. was standing at the bus station when boys threw bottles and ones broken glass flew up and cut leg BAD CUT. only about ten also, she says so must go and help as she is lost a husband recently too. I tell you no one knows how bad it is here with these children ALL OVER. They will be the death of us no mistake. also the world sitution no better, America Russia jews and Arabians irish and such. what can you do as it gets worse like one of yr poetry Works that I saw when cleaning desk with wax which I need more of soon as possible please. The same as in the empty tin. but well what can you do only get on with it. as you can't sort it all out can you? we are like the man in music Hall song that goes he plays his ~~Uku uker~~ Youkalaylee while the ship went down. only we all have problems like my sister and Goverments so can only carry on best we can, the next weeks money this week please as am short due to various things and the new wax pollish Viv.

PS. doctor said it is not SO bad but has had 6 stitch.

Glossy black slices of smooth slab are all laid facing towards due
East – in the twerpish conceit sunrise might pleasure them *now*!

Glittery gilt lists the names and the dates and the bullshit about
them
– 'Fell Asleep', 'Gone to Rest' (tcha!), 'Resting in Jesus' Arms'
(pah!).

'Gone Where We'll All Join Again on the Happy Shore Everafter'
(spew, vomit, puke, throw-up, retch), 'Went Without Saying
Goodbye'.

Inside a shed with the Council's coat-of-arms blazoned on it
there is a Flymo and spades. Here comes a gent with a pick:

'Wouldn't it make you want to dip your bread in the piss-pot
– some of the bilge they write there? Fuckin daft sods' (he opines).

Sweet peas are cunningly wrought in a huge pink crucifix resting
fresh on damp just-replaced turf. Wet clay outlines a new slot.

Biro-smudged sympathy-cards blow about and one is signed
'Viv, The
Depest Regrett Always Felt' (it shows a wren on a wreath).

On a diminutive gravy-hued sandstone wafer is chiselled
that which, despite mawkishness, prompts a sharp intake of
breath.

Aged 10.
Little Boy,
We Would Not
Wake You To
Suffer Again.

Oh sir,

only I havnt known. which way to TURN since the Funeral. It was the sisters youngest such a good lad too and only ten it seems wrong. somehow, and they would play in the streets though they was told often enough GOD only knows. So it was a bus when they was playing football and the poor little mite had gone when they got him. to the Hospitle so that is why I didn't come for 3 days but was in this morning and hope you find this note behind the tea pot and with thanks for the new Polish which have done the desk and chairs with. My oldest Trevor has been TOWER OF strenth since tragdy but <u>will</u> get those tatoos just like his DAD in that way just last week got MAM done on his hand which is nice he is a good lad to his Mother and a Tower. So can I have last weeks moneys though I did not come and not have money next week instead. Only the flowers which was a cross of pink flowers. very nicely done. do cost such a lot not that you bigrudge it do you when its your own Sisters youngest? So if you could leave it buy the dusters and furnature wax it will be fine tomorrow.

Obliged, Viv.

PS we take her to the zoo next weekend to take her out of herself. the sister. as it will be a nice change our Trevor says.

'Them animals is disgusting.'

In London Zoo is a large flat painted Disneyesque lion
sporting a circular hole cut where the face ought to be.

On its reverse is a step upon which the visitor stands and
puts his own face through the hole – so that he may be thus
snapped.

So, the resultant photograph shows the face of a friend or
relative grinning like mad out of a leonine frame.

This seems to be a very popular piece of equipment –
Arabs in nightshirts and Japs queue with Jews. Polaroids click.

Tabloids blown underfoot headline a couple of global débâcles.
Gran, from the lion's mouth, leers: toothless, cadaverous, blithe.

Oh it is very funny to put your head through the facial
orifice of a joke lion – races and creeds are agreed.

Down the old Monkey House there is a *Cercopithecus* wanking
and a baboon (with its thumb stuck up its arse) to revile.

Dear Sir didnt come in yesterday as planned as I lost key and how it happened was this. that we went to zoo with sister and the children which was the sister lost her youngest. And while we was throwing a ten pence for luck onto back of Allergator corcodile which is in Tropical House it must have fell from my purse. Everyone throws money for luck onto back of this Reptille and his pool is FULL of two P ten P and 5P pieces which bring GOOD LUCK to thrower. So had to go yesterday to see if the keeper had found it. he had and said they empty pool every month and spend money. It buys keepers there beer he says they get POUNDS so I got key back that is why I am here today instead but unfortunatly have by ACCIDENT spoilt one of your papers with poetry on it that was on yr desk as I threw it on the Parkray by mistake. and hope this is no inconvenience or can you do another one instead? Sister much better since outing but oldest boy Trev in trouble with police who came last night to house but I dont believe it as he is a good boy. But she is perking up a bit now and was cheerful at weekend and my boy took a Poloid Photo of her with head through a LION which was V. funny and makes her laugh which is good for her. Police say he has mugged but it canot be as he is GOOD BOY.

faithly VIV. p.s. worse things happen at SEA!

'Life is too black as he paints it' and 'Reading's nastiness some-
                                                                    times
seems a bit over the top' thinks a review – so does *he*.

Too black and over the top, though, is what the Actual often
happens to be, I'm afraid. He don't *invent* it, you know.

Take, for example, some snippets from last week's dailies before
                                                          they're
screwed up to light the Parkray: Birmingham, March '83,

on her allotment in King's Heath, picking daffodils, Dr
Dorris McCutcheon (retired) pauses to look at her veg.

Dr McCutcheon (aged 81) does not know that behind her,
Dennis (aged 36) lurks, clutching an old iron bar.

Unemployed labourer Dennis Bowering sneaks up behind her,
bashes her over the head – jaw, nose and cheek are smashed-in.

Dennis then drags her until he has got her into the tool-shed,
strikes her again and again, there is a sexual assault,

also a watch and some money worth less than ten pounds are
                                                        stolen.
'Is an appalling offence . . .' Bowering is told by the Judge.

Amateur frogmen discover a pair of human legs buried
Mafia-style in cement, deep in an Austrian lake.

Smugly, Americans rail over KA 007*;
angrily, Moscow retorts. Hokkaido fishermen find

* In September 1983 a Soviet fighter plane shot down a South Korean airliner when
all 269 passengers were killed, causing a brief stir.

five human bits of meat, one faceless limbless female Caucasian,
shirts, empty briefcases, shoes, fragments of little child's coat,

pieces of movable section of wing of a 747,
one piece of human back flesh (in salmon-fishermen's nets),

one headless human too mangled to ascertain what the sex is.
USA/USSR butcher a Boeing like chess

(probably civil jumbos *are* used for Intelligence business;
pity the poor sods on board don't have the chance to opt out).

Sexual outrage on woman of 88 robbed of her savings.
Finger found stuck on barbed wire. Too black and over the top.

Clearly we no longer hold *H. sapiens* in great reverence
(which situation, alas, no elegiacs can fix).

What do they think they're playing at, then, these Poetry Wal-
lahs?
Grub St. reviewing its own lame valedictory bunk.

dear Sir,

well I have hooverd and wax pollish the desk so I will collect money tomorrow. There is trouble on our block since my Tom plays the bones to tunes of George Formby and was due to give a TURN at the club tonight but was paralitic last night and WOULD try to practise and of course one of them. the bones. went over next door and the woman there that has the bitch that MARLD the child well her bitch grabs the bone but my Tom shouts abuse and. of course the outcome is there is a window broke. Which the man next door have only just mended after the last trouble. so we will see how it goes tonight at the Club he does that one he played his Youkerlaylie as the Ship Went down. and I know how He felt, because it is the same with my eldest Trevor who is REPRIMANDED IN CUSTARDY as the policeman put it who is a nice man but I know my lad is innerscent of that awful thing they say he done. But these things are sent to TRY Us as my Man says and I hope he plays his bones well tonight. just like he did that year we were in T.V. show Mr and Mrs, did you know we were in it? yes in Llandudno and he entertained the crowds they were in stitches when the ONE MAN BAND never turned up. so I have used up all the Johnsons Wax again so please oblige, We all have problems even the different Parlerments, also the police Forces. as well as me, and you with Yr writings.

Viv, P.S. we can only carry on the best we can manage

Down at the PDSA there's a queue of unprepossessing
buggered-up budgies and dogs. Someone is telling how Rex

quite unaccountably ('Never been known to act like it previous')
set on the nipper next door, and must now 'get put to sleep'.

'Even although he has done such a thing – and that to a kiddy –
I can't help loving him still – you *have* to stand by your own.'

'That's what I feels about my eldest (Trev) – they've done him for
mugging –
still, you *must* still love your own; if he's bad, he's *still* my boy.'

Cotton wool tenderly placed in a shoe-box comforts a frail life.
There is much love at the Vet's – even for bad dogs and Trev.

Was one time anchored in forty
fathom near unto the shore
of Mascarenhas Island.
Landed, we found blue pigeons
so tame as to suffer us
to capture them by our hands
so that we killed and roasted
above two hundred the first day.
Also we took many others –
grey paraquets, wild geese
and penguins (which last hath but stumps
for wings, so cannot fly).
Most entertaining to catch
a paraquet and make it
cry aloud till the rest
of its kind flocked round it and thus
enabled themselves to be caught.
Twenty five turtle, lying
under one tree, was taken.

On then to St Mary's Island,
where we careened, and thence
stood for the Straights of Sunda.

At 5° 30′
south of the line, the alarm
'Fire!' was raised – the steward
had gone below for brandy,
thrust candle into the hole
of a cask on the tier above
whence he drew his spirits, and when
removing his candle, a spark
had fell from the wick down the bung,
igniting the spirit. He poured
water unto the cask,

by which we had thought to choke it.

But the flames, reviving, blew out
the cask ends, when the fire
reached to a heap of coals
stowed there, which, lighted, gave off
a thick sulphureous smoke
thwarting attempts to extinguish it.

In this emergency
I appealed to the supercargo
to cast overboard all powder.
But (stubborn, arrogant, greedy,
as so many of his class)
he refused. Says he 'To throw
our powder away is to risk
attack from our enemies'.

Meantime the rage of the fire
augmented more and more.
We scuttled decks that greater
floods of water could be
got into ye hold, but all
attempts proved vain.

                    I resolved
to summon the carpenters
with augers to bore the hull
that water might enter below
and quench the flames.

                    But our oil
ignited then, d'ye see?,
and with sixty five good men
I stood on deck by the main

hatchway receiving buckets
when the powder, 300 kegs,
was reached.

　　　　　The vessel blew up
into the air with one hundred
and nineteen souls: a moment
afterwards, not one single
human being was seen:
believing myself to be launched
into eternity,
I cried out aloud for Mercy.

Some slender remnant of life
and resolution still lurked
in my heart. I gained the wreck,
as was gone to a thousand pieces,
clung to a yard.

　　　　　The long-boat,
got off afore the explosion
by a deserting faction,
now, in the very worst
of my extremity,
ran to the place with all speed,
whereat the trumpeter
threw out a line by which
I obtained that frail haven
of temporary ease,
and hymned being simply extant.

Cast up, one time, wrecked,
on bleak Patagonia
out of the Wager, Indiaman,
Commodore Anson's squadron.
Six years, afore we reached home.
Only food, shellfish and raw seal –
as we managed to stone unto death
or found dead, raw, rank, rotted.

Reduced thus to misery,
and so emaciated,
we scarce resembled mankind.
At nights in hail and snow
with naught but open beach
to lay down upon in order
to procure a little rest –
oftentimes having to pull off
the few rags I was left wearing,
it being impossible
to sleep with them on for the vermin
as by that time swarmed about them;
albeit, I often removed
my sark and, laying it down
on a boulder, beat it hard
with an huge stone, hoping to slay
an hundred of them at once,
for it were endless work
to pick them off one by one.
What we suffered from this
was worse even than the hunger.
But we were cleanly compared
of our captain, for I could compare
his body to nothing more like
an ant hill, so many thousand
of vermin crawling over it;

for he were past attempting
to rid himself in the least
of this torment, as he had quite
lost himself, not recollecting
our names that were about him,
nor his own. His beard as long
as an hermit's: that and his face
being besmirched of filth
from having been long accustomed
himself to sleep on a bag
in which he kept stinking seal meat
(which prudent measure he took
to prevent our getting at it
as he slept). His legs swelled huge
as mill-posts, whilst his torso
was as a skin packet of bones –
and upon bleached seal bones he played
hour after hour in uncanny
tattoo as to harmonize
with a wordless mindless dirge
as he moithered, moithered, moithered,
weird, xysterical airs,
yea, even unto the end.

Was one time cast on Oroolong,
when the Antelope packet went down.
The king of Coorooraa
succoured us, gave us meat,
in return of which we shewed him
the swivel as we had salvaged
out of the wreck, and the six-
pounder and our small-arms.
He and his natives were thrilled
and astonished. A flying squirrel
having settled upon a tree
nearby, our captain's servant
loaded his musquet, shot it.
Seeing the animal drop
off of a lofty tree's top,
without, apparently,
anything passing to it,
they ran to take it up;
when, perceiving the holes,
they chuckled, evidenced glee
and begged to be allowed
guns for themselves that they might
do slaughter of their near neighbours
whom they were desirous to see
fall, full of holes, as this,
dead in great quantity.
We acquiesced.

          They made
great execution with these,
our fire-arms, puzzling their foes,
who could not comprehend
how that their people dropped
without receiving any
apparent blow. Though holes

were seen in their bodies, they couldn't
divine by what agency
they were thus, in a moment, deprived
of motion and life. The whole
of the prisoners taken was shot.
We objected upon this last,
explained inhumanity
unto ye simple minds.

Their king gave unto us then
a kind of victory banquet,
whereat one tar of our number,
who out of the wreck had saved
an Italian violin
and had the bowing of it,
struck up. I know not whether
twas due to the victory,
or the feast, or to the grog
of which we allowed them a plenty,
or whether the fiddle musick;
but, be it whichever, they reeled,
cavorted like monkeys and fell
euphoric with our company
unto ye general dust.

Sailed one time aboard
trawler the Lucky Dragon,
crew o' 23,
hundred miles off Bikini,
in the March of '54.

Tars was all below
down in the a'ter-cabin;
crew man, Suzuki,
run abaft a-hollering
'The sun rises in the West!'

Hands mustered on deck,
saw, to larboard, a fireball,
like a rainbow brand,
rise up from ye horizon,
silent, that was the queer thing.

Minutes passed; the blast
suddenly shook the ocean,
shuddered our whole hulk,
hands was belayed with affright,
none, howsomdever, hurt (*then*).

But the skies turned *strange* –
misty wi' weird white ashes
as *swirled*, d'ye see?,
down onto decks, men, rigging . . .
That ash made us ill (*later*).

Most awful, terrific form
shipwreck can take is fire;
where the unfortunate
victims has only two
alternatives – to seek death
in one element in order
to avoid it in another.

One time the enemy's powder
(with whom we was close-engaged)
took fire – match left a-purpose
by their skipper, damn his eyes –
both the vessels blew up,
most violent dreadful explosion.

We, the spectators, ourselves
were the poor players also
in the bloody scene – some thinking
maybe it were the Last Judgement,
confounded, unable to gauge
whether or no we beheld it –
two ships hurled up on high
two hundred fathoms in air,
where there was formed a mountain
of fire, water and wreck;
dread conflagration below,
cannon unpeeling above,
rending of masts and planks,
ripping of canvas and cordage,
screams, like stuck pigs, of brent tars.

When the ship first took fire
I was blowed clean from the forecastle,
fell back into the sea
where I remained under water

unable to gain ye surface,
struggled as one afeared
of drowning, got up and seized
a bulk of mast as I found
nearby.

      Saw floating about
divers wounded and dead –
two half bodies, with still
some remnant of life, a-rising
and sinking, rising and sinking,
leaving the deep dyed pink.
Deplorable to behold
scores of limbs and fragments
of bodies – most of them spitted
on splintered timbers and spars.

Survivors we boarded a boat
almost entire from the wreck.
Most of us vomited constant
from swallowing pints of sea water.

I suffered long and swelled
to a surprising degree,
all my hair, face and one side
of my body were brent with powder;
bled at the mouth, nose, ears
(I know not whether this
be the effect of powder,
by swelling up the vessels
containing the blood of our bodies
to such extent that the ends
of the veins open and ooze it;
or whether it be occasioned
by the great noise and violent

motion in the same organs –
but let it happen which way
it will, there was no room there then
for consulting of physicians).

Thro the long night some sang,
attempting to keep up spirits.
Merciful Providence
preserving some measure of wine
and rum from the hold, the mate
contrived then to engineer
a musical instrument
on which he made bold to play.

Since I have so often felt
the malignant influence
of the stars presiding over
the seas, and by adverse fortune
lost all the wealth which, with such
trouble and care, I amassed,
it has been no source of pleasure
recalling to memory
the disasters that have assailed us.

Still, as a singer a song
or an old player an air,
I am impelled to convey
salt observations, a tar's
chantey habit, d'ye see?

I know not whether we've bid
adieu to the sea, or whether
we shall set forth again
where we have known such mischief;
whether traverse the ocean
in quest of a little wealth;
or rest in quiet and consume
what our relations have left us.

Our strange propensity
to undertake voyages,
alike to that of gaming –
whatever adversity
befalls us, we trust, at length,
prosperity shall o'ertake us,
therefore continue to play.

So with us at sea,
for, whatever calamity
we meet with, we hope for some
chance opportunity
to indemnify our losses.

And shall it, now, be counted
as ye dignified defiance
in us towards our fateful
merciless element,
or gull naiveté,
cousin to recklessness,
that, e'en in pitching Gulphward,
our salt kind brings forth chanteys?

Who would have thought it Sir, actually putting ME in a WRITING!
me and the Capting and ALL. What a turn up for the books.

Only, I must say I do not know HOW them people in poems
manage to say what they want – you know, in funny short lines,

or like what YOU do with them ones of yours sir, made of two lines like.
Still, when you're USED to it like, then you can speak natural.

Only, the newspaper man said that you was TRYING to sound like
low classes voices and that, only you wasn't no good –

you know, the CUTTING you left on yr desk top when I was waxing –
you know, that CRICKET which said you wasn't no good at all?

when you got TERRIBLE, stamping and raging calling him stupid
and how the man was a FOOL, which was the day you took DRINK.

'What is to one class of minds and perceptions exaggeration,
is to another plain truth' (Dickens remarks in a brief

preface to *Chuzzlewit*). 'I have not touched one character straight
from
life, but some counterpart of that very character has

asked me, incredulous, "Really now *did you* ever see, *really*,
anyone *really* like that?"' (this is the gist, not precise).

Well I can tell that old cricket that this is JUST how we speaks like,
me and the Capting and all (only not just in two lines).

One time, returning to home port, fell in with Englishman (16-
gunner) bound England from Spain; hailed her heave-to and
                                                          belay.

After a skirmish we forced her to strike her colours and seized
                                                          her.
Auctioned her off at Rochelle; carried the prize to Bordeaux.

Our tars had been so long absent from home that now we
                                                   indulged in
every extravagant vice, ere we be called to ye Deep.

Merchants advanced us, without hesitation, money and goods
                                                          on
promise of that which was our share of the booty, d'ye see?

We spent the night in whatever amusements best pleased our
                                                      fancy –
claret and gore and the stench of ye rank pox-festered trulls.

We spent the next day traversing the town in masquerade,
                                                      ranting,
had ourselves carried in chairs, lighted with torches, at noon.

As we caroused thus abroad we caused music, plucked forth
                                                  from gambas
boldly, t'embellish the raw, rude Dionysian debauch.

And the drear consequence of this gross wanton mass indiscre-
                                                          tion
was the untimely demise of damned near all the whole crew.

Jimmy 'The Beard' Ferrozzo, aged 40, Manager of the
Condor Club, where I now work (down San Francisco's North
Beach),

died when the stage-prop piano we used for Carol the stripper
pinned him tight into the roof, causing his breathing to stop.

Mr Boyd Stephens, the medical guy who did the autopsy,
said that Ferrozzo was pressed so tight he couldn't inhale,

said that 'Compression Asphyxia' is the name of the ball-game –
pressure had squashed up the chest so hard it couldn't expand.

I have been Caretaker down at the topless Condor Club now for,
must be a couple of years. When I unlocked, 9 a.m.,

I found Ferrozzo draped over his girlfriend (23-year-old
Trixie – this slag from the Club, nude Go-Go dancer, you know?).

She had no clothes on and she was stuck, screaming, under him
– it was
three hours before she could be freed by the cops from the raised

Steinway, a prop they have used at the Club for 2 decades almost
(topless star Carol descends, sprawled on the keys, to the stage).

Even now, no one knows what caused the joke piano to rise up
into the ceiling, 12 ft., pinning Ferrozzo and Trix.

Police say the motor that operates on the lifting device had
burned out and couldn't be switched so as to bring it back down.

Some way the Manager's body had kept her 2 or 3 inches
off of the ceiling and stopped Trixie herself being crushed.

Det. Whitney Gunther says: 'She was so drunk she doesn't
                                                    remember
laying down nude on the strings inside the grand – she just
                                                       knows

sometime that a.m. she woke up to hear the twanging of taut
                                                       wires.'
Man! What an Exit, you know? Welter of plucked gut and spunk.

Only, because it has broke (I.T.V.) we HAD to watch 'Seasars' –
stories about the roam Kings, dirty disgusting old lot.

One of them dressed up in smelly old skins and rushed out at captives
wounding there PRIVATES with KNIFE. also had LOVED his own
                                                       Mam.

this is called 'Narrow' which plays on a fiddle, all the time Roam burnd
but why it Brakes is because. my man has FIXED it last week

Also my mack is at cleaners because of kiddies which MARK it
ever so bad with their spit. They should be children of Roam –

what with the way they go on with their dirty, horrible, habbits
One of which made them all HEAR while he plays music all nite.

This one is known as 'Callegulum' which is v. funny name for
King but is THERE on t.v. So must be right. it is pink

leather effect with a belt and the reason why there is broken
glass on barometer is: cutting a LONG story short.

My man is playing it just as a banjo, being the SAME SHAPE,
singing the George Formby Song. and he has drop it on FLOOR.

SO that the glass and the silvery stuff you get in it all come
out and can not be got back. One of them SAWED men in half

also he has a poor soul stabbed to death with terrible pen nibs
also a mans' brains flogged out using a CHAIN for three days

which is the same sort of thing that you get in newspaper these days.
what with the Irish and that. so I have bought a new GAMP.

That is because of the Mack but he also made FATHER's go to
SEE their own kiddies killed dead, that was the worst thing of all

so it has broke and the needle now ALWAYS points to the STORMY –
he is a fool to have PLAYED (Formby) But ROAM is BAD TIME

Nero springs out girt in lynx pelts and slits slave's dick with a
razor . . .
ROAM is BAD TIME, as is Wolves: January '84,

19-year-olds Brian Johnson and friend Troy Blakeway are
jogging,
that they may catch the last bus, after a disco in town.

Leaving the Old Vic Hotel, Wolverhampton, they are pursued by
25 rampaging youths (West Indians, it appears).

Johnson leaps onto a bus but is stabbed twice just as the doors
close
(two deep long cuts in the thigh, 15 and 12 inches long).

At the Royal Hospital he receives more than seventy stitches.
Blakeway is knifed in the back, trying to flee from the mob –

in the deep 6-inch-long gash he gets thirty stitches; a sobbing
middle-aged parent attends (whose hand a nurse gently pats).

'Very sharp instruments must have been used for making these
nasty
injuries' C.I.D. says (Johnson and Blakeway concur).

It has not been without usefulness that the Press has adminis-
tered
wholesale mad slovenly filth, glibly in apposite prose,

for it has wholly anesthetized us to what we would either
break under horror of, or, join in, encouraged by trends.

Horrible headlines don't penetrate. Pongoid crania carry
on as though nothing were wrong. *Homo autophagous*, Inc.

**Gillian Weaver aged 22 walking 4-year-old daughter
home when a girl and three men** – hang on, this isn't just *news*:

Gillian Weaver aged 22 walking 4-year-old daughter
home when a girl and three men push her to pavement and steal

£3 from purse – she sits weeping and nursing 4-year-old (let's not
wax sentimental re kids; let's stick to facts, here *are* facts).

As she sits weeping and hugging her daughter, one of the
muggers
comes back and razors her thus **slashes her face 50 times**

(this is the *Mirror* and not my *self* – *I* have no axe to grind, right?)
**C.I.D. seeks three blacks plus one spotty, ginger-haired
white**.

Meanwhile, I've gotten the *5-Minute Uke Course* (Guaranteed
Foolproof) –
plinkplinka plinkplinka plonk plinkplinka plinkplinka plonk.

Grans are bewildered by post Coronation disintegration;
offspring of offspring of *their* offspring infest and despoil.

This is the Age Of The Greatly Bewildered Granny & Grandad,
shitlessly scared by the bad, mindless and jobless and young;

also the Age Of The Dispossessed Young, with nothing to lose by
horribly hurting their sires, babies and cripples, and whose

governments, freely elected and otherwise, function by mores
not altogether removed from their own bestial codes –

those sort of policies, that sort of hardware do not imply much
kindly respect for *H. sap*, mindless and jobless and young . . .

Maybe we're better off under the Civic Centre than up there
what with the LUTEing and that – them inner-cities is BAD,

maybe we're better off here in his WRITINGS, orrible though they
often is sometimes, than THERE – out in that awful real-life

what with its madness and sometimes I thinks the Capting's the only
sane one among the whole lot – Four or five leagues West-sou'west!

Steadily bear away under a reefed lug foresail, ye bilge rats,
synne rises firey and red – sure indycation o'gales,

we have entrapped us a sea-mew and served the blood to ye
                                                    weakest
members of crew, and myself? Liver and heart and ye guts.

For accompanying singing, the haunting harmony of the Uke has
no superior! Soft summer nights and the Uke are inseparable
pals! To wintry jollities the Uke adds zip and sparkle! Too much
mystery and confusion have shrouded Uke playing! The Uke is
an instrument for the best accompanying of happytime songs!
Beautiful and very unusual effects can be achieved! <u>You</u> can learn
to play richly harmonious accompaniments *in only a few minutes* by
this New Method, and when you have done that **you have
accomplished a great deal!**

'This is not Poetry, this is reality, untreated, nasty',
'This is demotic and cheap', 'This is mere caricature',

'This is just relishing violent, nasty . . .' so on and so forth,
Grub St. reviewing its own lame valedictory tosh –

Don't you go brooding and brooding and getting all of a state sir
just cos the LITARY GENT don't seem to like your nice books.

Like the old man used to always say 'When we wants YOU to chirp-up,
matey, we'll rattle the cage' – don't heed their old tommy-rot.

Grasp the pick lightly between thumb and first finger of right hand. Do not pinch! Move tip of pick back and forth across all four strings. Let that wrist hang loose! Start slow and then increase speed until you produce a smooth, even tone. Well done! The speed you move the pick across the strings will depend on what we call *tempo* (that means *time*) of the number you're accompanying! Well done! **That sounds just dandy!**

These are the questions that Councillors mean to raise at the
                                                            Meeting:
how much promethium remains? Has there been tritium used?

Why did the Army deny there was any contamination?
How do they mean to assure residents no risk remains?

What was the level of contamination? Where had it come from?
What is a 'low level' leak? Why was the public not told?

Why has the Army consistently issued flagrant denials
that any toxin remained after these secret 'events'?

Now you are ready for those oldies we know and love! Yes *Sir*! Sing, hum, or whistle the tune as you play! Play each chord as indicated until a new chord is shown. Do not change until you see another chord indicated! Everyone's just got to join in and **sing right along there!**

Carrying on as though things were O.K. is what we are good at – fall-out-proof bunkers are built, orbiting space stations planned.

Only, it's worse in the papers than what you stick in your writings, what with I seen a man knocked down WITH MY OWN EYES by black man and poor soul that was muged was ON CRUTCHES and that is gospel truth but not as bad as burning baby with CIG END which some swine done to get purse from mother of two. So even if they <u>are</u> out of work it is NOT RIGHT they should hurt their own townspeoples. Any road it is too late now so we can just HOPE FOR BEST which I DO, and will only live in shelter or outer spaces if there is no other possible. But will NOT eat sardines morning noon and night.

Finally now we return to the deep, and reaching our dim craft
drag her black hull through safe shale down to the fathomless
brine.

Next, to the dark-bellied vessel we carry white sails and main-
mast,
lifting aboard her the sheep, white tup and black ewe, and now,

heavily laden with misery, shedding tears in abundance,
hark to our skipper's command, nimble in wit and resource.

Thus we embark while astern of us rise up sail-swelling breezes
surging the blue-prowed ship forth, 12 knots with main-skysail
set.

So, d'ye see, after putting our gear and tackle in order,
all we can do is observe, course set by helmsman and wind.

Thus with full canvas we traverse the waters into ye blackness;
tenebrose, fog-bound, the bar, into the tow of the stream.

Here is perpetual smoke of a city unpierced by sunlight
where ye Cimmerians dwell, unvisible from above.

Here we make fast and drive up from the bilges, bleating, the
                                                    stunned sheep
into these bunkers of lead, granite and greyness and stench.

Wend your luff, messmates, and let go the skysail halliards,
                                                    mister,
cut the brace pennants and stays, reef the fore-topgallant in,

falling barometer, send down the skysail yard from aloft, sir,
strum with felt pick back and forth, lightly across all four strings,

all sail should be double-gasketted, stow the mainsail and cross-
                                                    jack,
make yr pentameters taut: two-and-a-half feet times two,

bend ye now three lower storm-staysails and a storm spanker,
                                                    mister,
take in the three upper tops, close-reef the foresail, F sharp,

tighten the B string and place finger at the back of the second
fret of the A string and keep spondees and dactyls close-clewed,

trim yr heroic hexameter (or it may be dactylic),
splice the pentameter aft, finger yr frets as ye go

surely we shouldn't be speaking like this sir, not in Allergic
Dis Talk, taint natural-like: I'm goin back to me prawse

only I've not been old self since they started the TREATMENT but do not
WORRY as they SWEAR it is non malingerent tumer ONLY which only
in my opinion only needs GOOD TONIC and will soon be old self again
but sometimes feeling bit on queer side that is to be expected the doctor say,
but what with one thing and another and the worry over eldest boy in trouble
with LAW I do not know which way to turn but I do wonder when you read
these cases what do the mothers think. and the father's. because they are all
some mothers children which loves them I should say. Even if they are vilent
crimnal. So will soon be back on feet again but this worry is worrying with
internashnal TROUBLE brewing as the BULLETIN says and I do not
feel so perky as previous. So will sign of for the present

if I could only be just this once pardoned Spawndies and Doctale
which we has never heard of down at the Ten-Storey-Flats.

The Triple Roll is one of the prettiest of all Uke strokes! It is a
very simple stroke too, when analyzed! Just follow the simple
stages below one step at a time! Soon you will get the 'knack'!
Yes, *Sir*!

Bring forefinger down across all four strings where neck joins
body of Uke. Bring that old fingernail down so that it glides
smoothly on the strings. That sounds just swell! Practise this
again and again and again! **Then follow with thumb down**.
After forefinger leaves last string bring ball of thumb down across
strings. **Then bring first finger up**. As thumb leaves last string,
bring the ball or fleshy part of forefinger up across all four strings.
Yes, *Sir*! Forefinger should begin to go up the very second that
little old thumb leaves the last string! Say! That sounds like a
million dollars! You, good buddy, have just mastered yourself the
TRIPLE ROLL!!!

I had believed myself fairly inured to foolishness after
6 months for Reuter's in parched mad bloody Lebanon, but

leaving the hotel that morning (with Dickie Pratt, of the *Mirror*),
in the main street of Sidon, I was presented with this:

out from the shade of the shelled former Admin. Offices stepped

                                                                    a
miniature, wielding a huge glinting black muzzle and stock,

just as a fat juicy jeep of Israelis swung into vision.
Three or four seconds he stood, sputtering hail at the jeep –

windscreen-glass frosted and one of the front seat occupants

                                                            oozed red,
there was a crackle of fire, ten or so seconds, and then,

as from a colander, into the pavement streamed out the juices
of the assailant, a slight soldier/homunculus. Well,

nobody looks for a *motive* from these old Testament shitters –
thick hate is still in the genes. I learned the boy was aged 12.

Say! At the outset, the beginner may find his finger just a little bit
stiff and clumsy but this disappears quickly after a little practice!
So why not keep right on along gut-pluck-a-plickin come rain or
come shine! Yes *Sir*! Let's start with the **little finger down** where
the neck joins the body . . .

'Tries to be shocking', 'Predictable, coarse, insensitive,

                                                        tasteless . . .'
when I want you to chirp-up, matey, I'll rattle the cage.

Say! What you need to do each day is keep that little Uke in tune!
Yes *Sir*! Who wants to hear an out-of-tune Uke? That's right! –
Nobody! Say! Why not tune that Uke right now? O.K. let's go!
You need a piano to help you. Tune A string to A on piano. Tune
D string to sound the same as D on piano. Tune F-Sharp string
and B string to sound like those notes on piano. Get it? If you do
not know where these notes are located on piano then ask some
guy who's a pianist to show you. Right?

What with the waiting and not knowing what on earth is the matter
up in the cities and that. Still, it was awful up there

what with last Wednesday that one what married him from the Top Flats
pushing the babby she was, down by the Preesint new shops,

suddenly found erself total surrounded by what-do-you-call-em?
them Rasterfastium blacks; you know, the ones with the LOCKS.

One got er purse but the pleece come and then the LEADER a FAT man
snatched up the babby and STABBED – right in the EYE with a pen,

animals that's what I think of them monsters horrible wild BEASTS
not safe to walk in the streets – not that we could NOW, of course

only it's funny for us being down here under the Civict
Centre – I thought it was all Underground Car Parks and that.

During this voyage ye heavens has been so dree overcast that
no observation by stars, nor yet by sun can be got.

Little round light like a tremulous faint star streams along
                                                    sparking,
blazes blue, shoots shroud to shroud, running along ye main
                                                    yard,

stays half the night with us, settles on fore-shrouds. Spaniards
                                                    call it
Fire of St. Elmo – be damned! Fire of ye Devil, it be.

Only the Capting gets mixed up about his time in the Navy –
muddles it up with them YARNS. You know, them ones what you READ,

not as I'm one for the books and that what with doing the housewort
(no Womans Libbance for ME, what with that much things to do.

get on with THIS Viv and THAT Viv and, well you has to LIVE don't
                                                    you?
that's what I think, any road). Close-clew your sails, mates, avast,

shew a reefed foresail to steer by and run for harbour my buckoes,
oakum discharged from hull's seams; pipe up all hands to the
                                                    pumps!

Make ye now ready for Davy Jones, messmates, get ye the
                                        strings tuned,
highest grade sheep's gut, they be – list to the boatman, belay,

as o'er the stream we glide borne by the rolling tide chanting and
                                        rowing . . .
Place your 3rd finger behind 3rd fret of 4th string and strum

Only I've never been happy but what I'm pottering, I ain't –
always the pottering sort, that's why I hates coming DOWN

mind you the Powertree Bloke and the Capting doesn't arf GABBLE –
what with the Capting his YARNS: tother keeps chaingin is VOICE

anyone'd think they was Everyone All Times Everywhere, way they
gabbles and rambles and that: still, they can't help it, poor souls.

Whatsisname says to me 'Viv you're the life and soul of the party' –
Viv, he says, MEANS life, you know (in Greek or Lating or French)

p̄linkp̆linkă|p̄linkp̆linkă|p̄linkp̆linkă|p̄linkp̄link|p̄linkp̆linkă|
                                        p̄linkp̄link
p̄linkp̆linkă|p̄linkp̆linkă|p̄lonk‖p̄linkp̆linkă|p̄linkp̆linkă|p̄lonk

Perduta Gente

South Bank: Sibelius 5's
incontrovertible end –
five exhalations, bray of expiry,
absolute silence...

Under the Festival Hall is a foetid
tenebrous concert
strobed by blue ambulance light.
PVC/newspapers/rags
insulate ranks of expendables, eyesores,
winos, unworthies,
one of which (stiff in its cardboard Electrolux
box stencilled **FRAGILE,
STOW THIS WAY UP, USE NO HOOKS**)
officers lug to the tumbril,
exhaling, like ostlers, its scents:

squit,

honk,

piss,

meths,

distress.

London's most exciting apartments
all have river views, £330,000 to £865,000

"Large homes standing in two or three acres are now selling for well in excess of £200,000," Mr Williams said.

"That means there is no shortage of people willing to pay a relatively high price for old barns so they can do them up. At the end of the day, they will have a substantial home set in several acres worth a good deal more than £200,000."

Derelict barns in south Shropshire are fetching six figure prices — and estate agents say there are no shortage of interested buyers.

A ruin at Eastham, near Tenbury, with no roof and hardly any walls is on offer for £100,000.

And an L-shaped barn with an acre of land near Worfield saw some fierce bidding between two developers before finally going under the hammer for £222,000.

Money is no object to buyers seeking a quiet country life.

A large barn at Cleobury Mortimer occupying a commanding position at the end of a mile long track has just sold for £90,000.

Another site at nearby Milson, involving the conversion of three barns standing on an acre of land, sold at £167,000.

One day a lone hag gippo arrived and
          camped on the waste ground
which we traversed on our way to the school bus
          every morning.

Cumulus breath puffs rose from a pink-nosed
          rope-tethered skewbald.
Winter: a frost fern fronded the iced glass
          caravan window
through which I ventured a peep, but I leapt back
          horribly startled
     when the rime cleared and an eye
     glared through the hole at my own.
(Filthy she was, matted hair, withered leg and
          stank of excreta.)

After that, each time we passed it we'd lob a
          rock at the window.
When it was smashed she replaced it with cardboard;
          one of us lit it -
she hobbled round with a pisspot and doused the
          flames with its contents.
Then she gave up and just left it a gaping
          black fenestration
     through which we chucked bits of scrap,
     rubbish, a dog turd, a brick.

     But when she skedaddled, a stain,
     delineating where she'd been,
     etiolated and crushed,
     blighted that place, and remained.

Now we arrive at the front of the ruin;
*   here are there moanings,*
*   shrieks, lamentations and dole,*
*   here is there naught that illumes.*
Mucky Preece lives in a pigsty beside the
            derelict L Barn,
        tetrous, pediculous, skint,
        swilling rough cider and Blue.
Now lie we sullenly here in the black mire -
*   this hymn they gurgle,*
*   being unable to speak.*
*   Here they blaspheme Divine Power.*
Money no object to buyer of L-shaped
**   picturesque old barn**
**   seeking the quiet country life**
        (two hundred and twenty-two grand,
        Property Pages last night -
        with which Mucky Preece is involved,
        scraping the squit from his arse).

terribly sick with her meths, but
she kept on and on vomiting through
the night, but with nothing left to
sick up (the front of her scraggy
overcoat covered in the methsy,
vegetable - soupy slime — the
stench abominable) so that
between honks she screamed hor-
ribly. The only sleep we got was
after one of the old hands dragged
her off, still screaming, and dumped
her in the alley round the corner
where the dustbins are.

Today is _Monday_: in St. Botolph's
crypt they give out free clothes to us

missiz an me inda warm inda Euston
          unnerground buskin
fugginwell busted armonica playin
          only da one fing
       over an zover again

missiz gone arse-over-ed on da fuggin
          down eshcalator
tryin to swing for some cuntinna bowler
          wot givver two pee
       bazshd up er face an er arm
       cetched up er sleeve in da fing
       where it gozsh clackety-clack
       mergency stop button presh

mashessa blood inna cetchup da coppers
          draggin er screamin
still wiv er good arm out of er pocket
          bockle uv Strongbow

gizzera fifty or twenny fer fuggsay
          mister a tellya
       savvy dis noosepaper see?
       sonly bed we gotter nigh

Remedy

Now that the hanging of murderers has been rejected by Parliament (myself I look upon hanging as barbaric) there is a simple alternative which will give the

They give them too much money to hang about the streets and not to look for work.

They should stop the dole money or cut it in half.

It would stop them

That remedy is to chop off his right leg and his left arm. After all, to give a prisoner a life sentence, he could be out in about 16 years.

EX-SOLDIER
(Name and address supplied)

EX-SOLDIER
(Name and address supplied)

— chop both his arms off. He couldn't do much with his feet.

We come to the person who goes to the dole office and states, by putting his signature to a piece of paper, that he is not working, that done, he then jumps into his car to do a 60 hour week.

The hand that puts his signature to paper should also be chopped off.

Some say they will fight on the beaches. It is a pity they weren't fighting during the war, a bit of army service would do them good.

Cut dole

cut

Gente perduta, wino-unworthies,
      knackered-up dipsos,
    swilling *rosato*-and-meths –
    we snooped a look in their lairs

while they were beachcombing: still-viscid meths-puke,
      faeces, a mattress,
    cardboard, an old plywood door,
    wedged in the clefts of the dunes.

Sweet from the pines wafts a resinous fragrance
      pungent with sea smells
    (molluscs, salinity, kelp);
    regular clank of a bell

tolls from a wreck-buoy, swung by the reflux;
      wardens in green jeeps,
    dapperly-uniformed, plump
    skedaddlers of squatters and tramps,

patrol what aspires to **Reserve of Endangered
      Natural Habitats**;
    a yellow and black JCB
    scrunches shacks into a skip.

author's last review which speaks of 'post-Chernobyl reindeer piled in a ruck in the tundra… trains with their burden of sinister finned flasks [rumbling] ominously on and on through a benighted city where trash amasses, the loonies and dispos [*sic* (presumably dispossessed)] proliferate and the resident strumpet of the Globe opines "If you ask me, this planet is fucked; not just me, love, the whole planet, fucked".' This, scribbled as circumstances permitted, between the derry (derelict house) and St Botolph's crypt where the destitute alcos

102

today. I got some trousers but they had very bad stains down the front and the knees were both in tatters and they stank. The woman in front of me got a yellow vest but said she could see lice and fleas in it and called the vicar a fucking cunt.

Tuesday: In the crypt of St. Botolph's we got a mug of tea and some bits of bread. It's like a sort of air-raid shelter with us all waiting for something awful to go away, or, worse, to happen.

Friday 19th: got some Strongbow with this old shitty dosser, blake

Snarl of a JCB, cordon of Old Bill,
      megaphone rasping
    into a 3 a.m. squat.

Sleep-fuddled dissolutes, still dressing cold dis-
      consolate bratlings,
    struggle with carrier-bags.

One of the Council Bailiffs is sporting a
      Have a Nice Day badge
    fixed on the yellow hard hat.

Often at dusk in the birch woods beyond the
        gates of the city,
you see the glimmer of fires of the hapless
        dispossessed losers.

One of these, russetly lit from beneath by
        fulminant embers,
    howls through the tenebrous gloom -
    something concerning smoked fish,
    black bread and vodka, I think.

Distant, a plangently-played balalaika ac-
        companies wailing
    vocals whose burden is loss -
Gone are the youthfully beautiful whom I
        loved in my nonage;
    strength and vitality, gone;
    roof-tree and cooking-hearth, gone.

Eyes like an elephant's, blood-bleared and tiny,
        gowkily ogle;
tremulous wart-knuckled pachyderm fingers
        fumble a tin cup;
skewers of carp flesh fumed to mahogany;
        dark-crusted rye loaf;
    sloshed spirit hissing in ash.

who, like me, is no stranger to the
pig-pen o' nights, told me how he went
to the Spike last night, but was so
rough still from the surgical spirit
that he fell down the stone stairs and
smashed his face up badly. They told him
to fuck off and come back when he
was better. He did a Skipper last
night on the kitchen window-ledge
of the Royal Hotel — you get a bit of
warmth through the glass — but
the police came round and moved
him on. <u>Tues 23rd</u>: The same bloke I was
on about yesterday got given a quid,
so we got this tin of Carlsberg Sp

Don't think it couldn't be you –
      bankrupted, batty, bereft,
huddle of papers and rags in a cardboard
            spin-drier carton,
bottle-bank cocktails and Snow soporifics,
            meths analgesics,
beg-bucket rattler, no-hope no-homer,
            squatter in rat-pits,
      busker in underground bogs
      (plangent the harp-twang, the *Hwaet!*
Haggard, the youthful and handsome whom I
            loved in my nonage;
      vanished, the vigour I valued;
      roof-tree and cooking-hearth, sacked).
      Bankrupted, batty, bereft –
      don't think it couldn't be you.

gizzera quiddora fiftyfer fuggsay
       mistera tellya
tellya da missiziz fugginwell whatnot
       fugginwell ampute
    afer da nackerup arm

armazzerfuggerup der inda Euston
       afera go down
    arse-over-ed in da fing
    waz ish osh clackeshy-clig

missiziz gointer ospical ad da
       whassizname tashun

    tashun da arm as iz skwozsh
    cuts ov da armaziz skwozsh
    nowizza bagwiv one arm
    ospical calls amputaysh

and have been not infrequently
covered in the crusted slurry of the bare
beasts with whom I had shared a night's
accommodation.

At about this time yesterday, the St.
Mungo's crowd came round on the soup
run. Nuns called the Poor Sisters of the
Mother of God, or some such crap, dish-
ing us all out with plastic cups of
thin brown broth and a couple of slices
of day white Mother's Pride. One of the
blokes under the fly-over climbed into
the van and got his dick out. He's
a Brasso addict and was sick
all over the chief nun and

That one is Boris the Swine
(known as 'the Swine' for the fact that he sometimes
          falls in the swine-pen
     when he is terribly drunk –
     covered in slurry for days),
but we must make allowances, since he
          worked at the Station
     when the — remember the headline
(**Efforts are now being made to encase the
          damaged reactor**)?

Often at evening he plangently strums and
          bays from the birch wood,
     where he reposes, this strain:
     Nothing can ever be done;
     things are intractably thus;
all know the bite of grief, all will be brought to
          destiny's issue;
those who have precognition suffer
          sorrow beforehand;
bodies are bankrupt, the main Expedition has
          left us behind it.

Acute Exposure
(Gamma Rads)

Widespread experimental work with m has confirmed the volatile nature of fission p fault conditions. This was discussed more ful concluded that for the purpose of overall asse assume that the gaseous and volatile fission p tions relative to one and other in which they xenon, iodine, tellurium, caesium and rutheniu fission products of importance. From the expe not appear to be volatile in the conditions of reasonable accord with the evidence and a reas to take the release of strontium isotopes, exp activities of the isotopes present in fuel, as assumed for the release of gaseous and volatil activities of important fission products prese fuel are given in Table II of Lecture No. 6.

DISPERSION OF RADIOACTIVITY IN THE ATMOSPHERE

3. Pasquill's method of calculating the in the atmosphere is in use in the U.K.[1]. I known theoretical treatment by Sutton[2] to gr empirical correlation of measurements made to

January, 2 a.m.:
at roost on the window-ledge outside a hotel's
        kitchen a dirty
    hirsute in three overcoats
snuggles against frosted glass where a cabbage-
        smelling Vent-Axia
    sussurates vestigial warmth.

Muezzins were Tannoying dirgefully from the
            mosques in the fountained
squares of the Turkish end of the city;
            barbecued goats' smoke
            swealed from ramshackle cafés.

Stallholders (leather and pewterware) tweaked the
            sleeves of the wealthy
Euro/American/Japanese gawpers
            thronging the cramped wynds;
            fezzed coffee-drinkers played chess.

Squatting in alley-muck, whining, a woman
            cradled a frail child;
two other infants with counterfeit blindness,
            rattling beg-bowls,
            obediently foamed at the mouth –

manifest mendicant mountebanks (though their
            glee was authentic
            when you disburdened yourself
            of that frayed ten-dinar note).

Worse than the Shakes is the Horrors — the rats and
        echoing voices...

        echoing voices
under the flyover, rubble and streets of
        boarded-up derries –
No Go for ambulance, fire-brigade, milkman,
        Post Office, Old Bill...

    when they demolished his sty
    Mucky Preece, alias Tucker,
    tramped from the sticks to the Borough –
    his mother was only a gippo,
    his only possession a bucket...

sometimes it seems like a terrible dream, in
        which we are crouching
    gagged, disregarded, unsought
    in dosshouses, derries and spikes,
    and from which we shall awake,

    mostly it seems, though, we won't.

iernobyl ac

Unit 4 of the Cher-
c Soviet Union is the
has ever occurred at a
lant, in several respects:
f human casualties, in the
released, in the
-strained

14 speech on the
tion confirmed th
week earlier by a
the International /
that the initiating
excursion within t
At the time of th
was at a power le
or 200 MWt. Since
he first two victim
adjustor of a
erator of
ns l

Some workers must have got their skin
contaminated while removing their out
the vault.   Improper handling of commu
contamination.   From there, the contam
areas around Unit 1 including the Retu
other workers.

Radioactive contamination in the air

a.   Particulate (or dust)

b.   Vapour - Iodine, $1H^3$

c.   Gaseous - Argon-41, Xe-135, Kr-88

Particulate activity is measured by co
a high efficiency filter and counting
Continuous monitors are of two types.

could have expected that the author himself would have plumbed such depths of filth, depravity and degradation. For, indeed by his own account (the MS Diaries, pp.101–113), he was by this time: 'no stranger to the pig-pen o'nights'; 'not infrequently covered in the crusted slurry of the base beasts with whom [sic] [he] had shared a night's accommodation'; 'acquainted with the subtleties of the Bottle–Bank Cocktail, the urinous scent of the squat, the needle's brief oblivion, grief's bite'.

And then, to the indescribable squalor of

Under the concreted cantilevered
            haven of arty
        spans of the *Bibliothek*,
shivering dossers each evening repose in
            newspaper bivvies.
        Mornings, they head for the park.

Slats of the frost-crusted park benches steam in
            8 a.m. sunlight.
        Scavenging corvine-clawed men
rifle each *Abfalleimer*, greedily
            glean after rye crusts
        flung for gross ducks near the lake,

swig the sour dregs of the bottle-bank empties,
        Tafelwein, Schaumwein,
        Spätlese, Steinhäger, Schnapps.
Today I have planted a two-kilo *Schinken*
            where they will find it
        [hooray for the secular saint].

Course ee woz always the Black Sheik of the
        family, ee woz,
     went to une versity too
     (done moths an physicals there),

ad a good job ee did too with that Anat-
        omical Engy,
     then ee dripped out on the dole,
     got on the booze an them dregs

(cococo whatsisname, you know, the white stuff),
        now ees a squitter,
     lives in a squit with no rent,
     eed ad a radio dose.

How doeth the citie sit solitarie that
            was full of people?
She that was great among nations hath no
            comforter, all her
        friends haue dealt treacherously.

Something is in the air, more and more nutters,
            alcos and dossers,
            dole diuturnal.

Sometimes it seems like a terrible dream from
            which we'll awaken;
        but mostly it seems that we won't.

Let us descend, though, through urinous subways to
            miseries greater,
al doloroso ospizio, where the
            newly tormented
            sample new torments.

    Woe vnto them that decree
    vnrighteous decrees and that turn
    the needy from iustice and robbe
    the rights from the poore of my people.

    What will ye doe with yr wealth
    in the day of the storme which shall come
    from afarre, when all that remaines
    is to crouch with those ye haue oppressed?

te Whole Body Doses

	Probable Effects
	detectable clinical effects. bbably no delayed effects.
	ight blood changes with later covery. Possible nausea. layed effects possible but cious effects improbable.
	usea and fatigue, possible omiting. Reduction in certain lood cells with delayed recovry.
	Nausea and vomiting on first lay. Two week latent period followed by general malaise, loss of appetite, diarrhea, moderate emaciation. Possible death in 2-6 weeks but for most healthy individuals, recovery likely.
	Nausea, vomiting, diarrhea in first hours. Short latent period followed by epilation, loss of appetite, general malaise, then hemmorrhage, emaciation, purpura, diarrh--

`~`ammatio of throa`+`

first

Most of them quietly left when the Council
        put in the Bailiffs
        (3 in the morning it was);
        but one nutter stayed there holed up,

stuck his head out of the fourth-storey smashed-paned
        window and hollered
        Don't think it couldn't be you.
        Then he began chucking rats –

ten or a dozen big dead ones (the squat was
        full of them, we found,
        when we moved in with the dozers).
        Queerest thing of the lot

was he came to the window and empted a briefcase
        full of these *papers*,
        hundreds of fluttering sheets
        caught in the wind off the sea,

shipment of radioactive materials,
        health implications,
        Smear Meter, that sort of stuff
        printed on pages ripped out,

radiological half life, atmos-
        pheric dispersal,
        Gamma-fields, Carbon-14,
        blown through the dead silent Borough.

These who have never lived, blind lives so mean they
envy all others,
caitiffs whose deep-wailing plaints,
horrible outcries, hoarse sighs,
Even in duff weather I'd rather do a
skipper than stop there –
trouble of kiphouses is
vermin and no privacy.
piercing the starless air, dark-stained, dolent;
when I remember,
terror still bathes me in sweat –
their thunderous outbreathing of woe.
Hundreds of beds and the blankets is never
changed off the last one –
crabs, you can pick up like that.
No fucking plugs in the sinks.
From the tormented Sad, sigh-troubled breath a-
rises around them,
crowds that are many and great,
children and women and men.
Bloke in the next bed to me (I could see him)
pissed in his pillow
then he just slep on it wet.
Some on em masturbates, loud.
Let us not speak of them, merely observe and
silently pass by.

Isotope	
I-131	
Cs-137	
Sr-90	
Ru-106	910 rad lung dose to a 6 month old child

inversion ....

the present Lecture, the cloud-dosag(

5×10^{-5} curie-sec/metre^3. Therefor(

dosage of gamma activity would be

$$2 \cdot 011 \times 10^6 \times 5 \times 10^-$$

The dose from a semi-infinite cloud w

according to formula (2). From figur

size of the cloud is $0 \cdot 38$. Hence the

cloud would be

$$25 \times 0 \cdot$$

Again, from Table II of Lecture No. 6

be $0 \cdot 521 \times 10^6$ curie-MeV. Therefore

filters which retained all the iodine

gamma radiation dose would be reduced

EXTERNAL RADIATION FROM ACTIVITY DEPO!

a radiological half life of 5700 years.

a long, long time. Carbon-14 emits a l

of 156 keV. It emits no gamma ray. Th

After the meths she was honking and honking –
     front of the frayed mac
    stippled with vegetal bits,
    Surgical Spirit-beslimed.

In between honks she was screaming and screaming –
     someone has dragged her
    out of the derry back door,
    dumped her where we piss and shit.
    Now we can all get some kip.

or at least seems very likely, that he was given, we do not know by whom, a parcel of 'inside' papers relating to safety procedures during reactor damage and the 'black dust' scare. Since the authorities regarded all matters concerning environmental contamination as Official Secrets, the author's possession and publication (albeit in a form artistically metamorphosed) of certain of these documents was something of a risk. He steadfastly maintained to the police that he had found the material in a trash bucket on the Victoria Line station where he was busking.

That he was now physically and financially derelict ('No stranger to the unstemmable welter of shit') seems to have concentrated his notion of the 'slurry-wallowing degraded dispossessed' as a metaphor for all of *H. sapiens* involuntarily subjected to that other 'excreta' and thereby, irrespective of position in society, dispossessed of

Outside Victoria Station a quorum of
　　　　no-hoper foetid
impromptu imbibers is causing a shindy:
　　　　one of the number,
clutching a bottle of Thunderbird, half-full,
　　　　rolls amongst litter
(chip-papers, Pepsi cans, Embassy packets –
　　　　Indian take-out
　　remnants adhere to her mac);
　　under one arm is a crutch
　　(the other is lopped at the elbow);
plaster encases her leg, which a colleague
　　　　(sipping a Carlsberg)
kicks periodically, bellowing 'fugg-bag,
　　　　fuggbagging fugg-bag'.

1. Radiation Protection

7. Contamination Control

1. Personnel Movement Control

INTRODUCTION

Radioactive contamination may spread f
another in various ways. One of the princi
moving into a contaminated area and trackin
material on their clothing, shoes and perso
Various movement control techniques have ev

RADIATION EMERGENCY PROCEDURES

title

Hazard Identification

radiation hazards present in the shutdow
those normally present and those having p
ng retubing activities, are:

Ambient Gamma-fields

mination residing on the interior of pip
ated components and fuel within the react
1 shutdown conditions. These fields resu
nt Gamma-fields are found within the reac

Radiation Beams Originating from the

gical shielding normally provides effec
iated with the activated in-core compo
as intense as 300 R/H, may emanate fr
al of a shield plug (S/P) from or of a

Radiation Fields Originating fror
Components and Fuel Removed from

Newspaper, wrapped round the torso between the
            fourth and fifth jerseys
(night attire proper for doing a skipper in
            icy December
        under the Festival Hall),
carries a note to the Editor, from 'Ex-
            Soldier' of Telford,
        outlining plans to withdraw
        DHSS cash from those
        no-fixed-abode parasites.

Wound round a varicose indigo swollen
            leg, between second
        and third pair of trousers (which stink –
        urine and faeces and sick),
Property Pages delineate *bijou*
            River-View Flatlets
        £600,000 each.

How much promethium remains?
Has there been tritium used?

Why did the PM deny there was any
        contamination?
    How do they mean to assure
    home-owners no risk remains?

What was the level of contamination?
        Where had it come from?
    What is a 'Low Level' leak?
    Why was the public not told?

Why has the PM consistently issued
        flagrant denials
    that any toxin remains
    after these secret 'events'?

These are the questions which residents meant to
        raise at the Meeting,
    had it materialized.

113

of the Bottle - Bank cocktail. As
we guzzled this mixture of stuff from
the empties (shaken up in a wine bottle
— a bit sour but OK, only it made us
sick afterwards) he said he used to
work at some atomic power station
(quite posh, he was) but he got the
sack for telling the newspapers about
some radio-active leak, and he'd
stolen all these papers — Top-Secret
— from the Power Station, and he
couldn't get work and then his
wife died (cancer) so he came to
this. I think he was fucking
well crackers, but we all

Week of continuous Blue,
total amnesia, no recollection of
          date or condition,
      skipper or kiphouse or spike,
      contusion and blood on the scalp,
      spew, epilation, the squits,
sight as through flawed glass, misted, contorted,
          nuns from St Mungo's
      doling out dry bread and soup,
      Mucky Preece skinning a cat
      (bashed-in its head with a brick)
      to add to the vegetal stew
      bubbling up in the bucket,
swayingly unzips and waggles his penis,
          smirched with the cat's gore,
urinates into the face of a Blessed
          Sister of Mercy.

[And don't think it couldn't be *you*:
grievously wounded veteran of the
Battle of Bottle,
jobless, bereft of home, skint,
down in the cold uriniferous subway
spattered with drooled spawl,
lying in layers of newspaper ironies –
Property Prices,
smug To the Editor platitudes on The
Vagrancy Issue,
ads for Gonzalez Byass;
dosser with Top Man carrier-bag, en-
swathed in an *FT*;
Gizzera quiddora fiftyfer fuggsay,
bankrupted, I been,
fugginwell bankrupted, me;
dolent, the wail from the Tube;
and don't think it couldn't be *you*.]

and 'morose old hypochondriac', as one reviewer dubbed his literary persona — which projected affectation was to become increasingly the reality.

During those last months of inebriate degeneracy (spent under the concrete span of a flyover, in an abandoned skip and in a defunct fibreglass storage bunker — sometime repository of the Borough's rock-salt for icy winter streets), the burden of his monody, rarely coherent, seems to have been Black Dust, 'Pancake' Contamination Meters, Smear Meters, Clean Zones and stochastic risk and

RIVER VIEWS FROM £123,500

VELVET CURTAINS

Sheds

KENNELS

MAINTENANCE FREE
STORAGE CONTAINERS

Back of the Maximart, Saturday evenings:
        sometimes they chuck out
edibles (Sell By or Best Before dates of
        which have expired –
    Cheese n' Ham Tasties, Swiss Rolls,
    Ready-to-Microwave-Burgers)
into a skip in the alley.
Tonight it is minty ice-cream.

Icy December: three rank expendables
        squat on a split tomb
    covered in carroty spew.
one has his cock loose and pisses all over him-
        self and his colleagues –
    steam from both this and their breaths.
Each grasps a 2-litre polythene tub from
        which is extracted
scoopings of green ice by black half-mooned fingers.
        Slurping and beard-smirch,
    guzzle and emerald puke,
punctuate pulls from the communal Blue of
        methyl amnesia.

Wind that disperses the Cloud is a blow for
       Federalism,
fairly enfolding Muskovite, minaret,
       Einkaufszentrum.

Scoffing our tea, bread-and-marge and secreted
       surgical spirit
here in the crypt of St Botolph's it feels like a
       fallout-shelter.

Functional Disturbance of the Gut Fo

After irradiation of the gut in
following disturbances of general fu:
one to two hours:

(1) Nausea and vomiting

This might be thought of as a "r
which stomach contents are dispo
handled by the normal digestive
bably originates in the brain.

(2) Diarrhoea

This is also a rejection phenome
mechanisms.

it was discovered that some of the staff
ject had radioactive contamination on their
estigation it became evident that this form
tected by our "Pancake" contamination meters,
"smear" meters, but not by our older field
foot monitors, nor by the portal monitors.

Please find attached a status report
place
number of workers on the Large Scale
had contamination on their skin and c
the hand and foot monitors

Carbon-14 Contamination Problem

Melted-down boot polish, eau de Cologne, meths,
        surgical spirit,
    kerosine, car diesel, derv...

When the St Mungo lot roll up with hot soup,
        what you should do is
    keep back the slice of dry bread;

after they've fucked off, plaster the one side
        thick with the Brasso –
    goes down a regular treat.

    After a gobble of meths,
    crunch up a Trebor Mint fast –
    takes off the heat and the taste.

Piled in a ruck in the tundra a tump of
        Geigering reindeer...

Meanwhile the trains with their sinister finned flasks
        carrying spent rods
    hurtle perpetually on
through the benighted cities where trash a-
        masses and loonies,
alcos and other misfortunates make dole,
        one of whom ventures:
    I think this planet is fucked;
    not just me but the whole planet, fucked.

that she was into the _lot_ — she
kept on about H and Coke and D.D.A.s
and skin-popping and main-lining
and then, when we started to have this
stew I'd made out of the rotten vegetables
they throw away off the stalls in the
market, she threw up straight in
the fire — we'd got a fire going in
the derry, made out of all the
banisters in the house. Then
someone shouted that the Bailiffs
were coming with the dozers,
and we got all the rats that we'd
killed, and got ready to chuck
them at those bastards with the

Legions of comatose owners of nothing
       under the concrete
   arches are juddered awake,
   impotent, dolent, bereft –

   radioactive spent rods,
bound for reprocessing from the reactors,
      carried in finned flasks,
rumble by railway by night through a city
      hugely unconscious.

   Nothing can ever be done;
   things are intractably thus;
knowing the bite of grief, all will be brought to
      destiny's issue;
those having precognition suffer
      sorrow beforehand.

Grief-bitten impotent owners of nothing,
      holding opinions
   gagged, disregarded, unsought.

Something is in the wind: terrible storms, an
                absence of ozone,
        huge decommission of plants,
        delapse and delapse and delapse...

        10,000 undesired drums
        (3,800 tonnes)
abandoned four-high in a rickety stack that
                pops with expansion,
        sizzles and bubbles and fumes
        fizzing from leaks in the rust
        in the full glare of the sun
200 yards from a shanty camp's tetrous ex-
                pendable tosspots,
        scumbags and alcos and bums.

how the author was last encountered in the concourse of Euston, pediculous, intoxicated beyond capability, plunging and bucking like a demented warhorse — the side of the head oftentimes cracking against the tiled floor, blood and contusion already in evidence, a (profoundly embarrassed and irritated) companion struggling to hold

Council blokes pulled down the derry and then set
        fire to the floorboards,
rafters and anything else that would burn (the
        squatters of course had
     already burnt all the doors,
      banisters, skirtingboards, stairs).

Those who had formerly dossed there returned that
        night to the bonfire,
Mucky Preece found an old bucket and stewed up
        veg which the market
stallholders chuck in the gutters because it's
       rotten or damaged –
      onions, a turnip, some sprouts.
      The embers were glowing for days.

That's where they found it, singed to the waist, its
        charcoaly leg-sticks
(one of which must have been smashed and remained en-
        cased in cast plaster)
      stuck in still-fulminant ash,
      bits of veg puked on the mac,
      blue meths clutched tight in one claw,
      other limb lopped at the elbow.

Wind that disperses the Cloud (a blow for De-
            mocracy) favours
Palace twerp, propertied yuppie and news-wrapped
            dosser with doses
equal in Geiger croaks. Shreds of (marked **Secret**)
            papers are scuttering
      over the wrecked party-lawn's
      panic-vacated marquee
      and under the Festival Hall,
      drift against cheap sleeping-bags,
      cardboard, plonk bottles and stiffs:

                              rads,

                              stront,

                              risk,

                              leak,

                              contam

Health Implications

Based on the risk estimates
can be concluded that the ri
cancer after irradiation to
from negative to an upper bc
year per rem (Section 2.1).
mulation of extremity dose t
lifetime, it can be shown th
skin cancer is 2.4×10^{-5} pe
risk, based on the 5% case-f
1.2×10^{-6} per rem which is
of the total stochastic risk
Therefore, our calculation i
ICRP's skin weighting factor

inr.   .c. Some
deaths in .   .. weeks, possible
eventual death of 50% of indi-
viduals for about 450 rads.

Nausea, vomiting, diarrhea in
first hours. Short latent
period followed by diarrhea,
hemorrhage, purpura, inflam-
mation of throat, fever by
end of first week. Rapid ema-
ciation, and death as early as
2nd week with possible eventual
death of 100% of exposed indi-
viduals.

approved by

Carrying on as though nothing is wrong is
        what we are good at:
        incontrovertible end;
        shrieks, lamentations and dole;
        lost livers, roof-trees and hearths;
on the waste ground at the back of the factory
        there's a crone scumbag
        that kips in a big cardboard box,
        etiolated and crushed;
those having precognition suffer
        madness beforehand
(**Efforts are now being made to encase in
        concrete the...**); meanwhile,
here is a factory daily producing
        thousands of badges
        emblazoned with **Have a Nice Day**.

Dusty, crepuscular, vast;
ranks of unfortunate supines fading
    into infinity;
  chamber or bunker or vault
seemingly lacking extremities; coughing,
    puking, diarrhoea;
drone of the crazy invisible exe-
    getist intoning
  Woe vnto woe vnto woe
  vnto woe vnto woe vnto woe

squit
rats

honk
strut

piss
risk

moths
leak

dis   tress
con   tam